Awesome Riddles

for

Awesome Kids

By

Myles O'Smiles

Cataloguing in Publication Data

Myles O'Smiles

Awesome Riddles for Awesome Kids

Description: Crimson Hill Books trade paperback edition | Nova Scotia, Canada

ISBN 978-1-988650-65-4 (Paperback)

BISAC: JNF028020 Juvenile Nonfiction: Humor - Jokes & Riddles | JNF021050 Juvenile Nonfiction: Games & Activities - Questions & Answers | JNF021070 Juvenile Nonfiction: Games & Activities - Word Games

THEMA: Y - Children's, Teenage & Educational | YPC - Educational: Language, literature & literacy | YNU - Children's / Teenage general interest: Humour & jokes

Record available at https://www.bac-lac.gc.ca/eng/Pages/home.aspx

Illustrations: Camilo Luis Berneri
Book design and formatting: Jesse Johnson

Crimson Hill Books
(a division of)
Crimson Hill Products Inc.
Wolfville, Nova Scotia
Canada

AWESOME RIDDLES FOR AWESOME KIDS is a children's word game book. It has riddles and tricky questions to entertain and delight kids plus silly and funny cartoon illustrations.

Readers ages 8 to 12 and older will enjoy reading and sharing these riddles and their answers. They'll also learn how to create their own riddles and trick questions!

Riddles are a fun way to improve reading, communication and social skills for young readers, new readers, ESL students and anyone who likes to play with language!

All these riddles are kid-pleasers and family-friendly! Hours of fun for everyone!

Do you know what I could be,
hidden here for you to see?

Hey, don't peek at the answer just yet!
Put your thinking cap on and the answer you'll get.

I might be silly or serious. I might be a rhyme.
I might be something that's funny any old time.

I describe something you know; you might use it today.
Or I might have numbers for words, a game of wordplay.

If you've already guessed what I could be,
it's time for the answer to the question of me.

What am I?

A riddle.

Note to Teachers & Parents

Why Kids Need Riddles

Hello, Myles O'Smiles here, with some questions for you.

Do you remember the very first riddle you ever heard in your life?

Or the very best riddle anyone ever told you when you were a kid?

Or the best riddle you've heard recently?

Possibly. But it's more likely that you remember the pleasure of that riddle. The moment of surprise. The smile and maybe the laugh that followed.

Riddles present creative, intriguing and entertaining ways of describing things everybody is familiar with. Sometimes the riddle clues are meant to mislead, or there are double-meanings.

Riddles are known for their metaphors, spinning fancy (and possibly misleading) descriptions of common objects.

Riddles can also be rhymes, but they don't have to be.

People have created, enjoyed and shared riddles for untold thousands of years. The ancient Greeks revered riddle-writing and riddle-telling as demonstrations of sparkling wit and good humour. Shakespeare included dozens of riddles in his plays.

Watch any children's animated movie or listen to just about any engaging speech and chances are you'll spot how they use riddles to charm and engage their audiences.

Even in our modern world, with all our technologies and diversions, riddles still have the power to make people of all ages pause, think, and smile.

Riddles can do more than simply entertain us. If you're a teacher or a parent, you can use riddles to lighten the mood, change the subject, stimulate creative and analytical thinking, build communication skills or as a reward for tasks completed.

Riddles can be great conversation-starters, ice-breakers and beginnings or endings to almost any speech or presentation. Knowing how to share them is a social skill that can help build confidence.

The riddles in Awesome Riddles for Awesome Kids are designed for people ages 8 to 12, but they're also relevant for students of all ages, encouraging reluctant learners, ESL students and mature students.

Both as a parent and former teacher, I believe everything we give our kids needs to be real-world and empowering. This means no meanness, no insults, no cursing and no adult content. Just good, clean fun. That's what you'll find in this book and all the books in this series. In this one, there are riddles and tricky questions to intrigue, challenge and delight kids.

So here you are…Enjoy!

Myles O'Smiles

Note to Kids

Having Fun With Riddles

Riddles can be silly.

Or not.

Funny.

Or a fact.

Maybe they rhyme.

Or they don't.

But what ALL riddles do is ask a tricky question, about something the other person already knows about. That's where the fun is – seeing if you can be tricked or trick someone else, with a clever riddle!

You could just read this book, and that's fine. But here's a way to play a riddle game that's even more fun!

I call it being RIDDLE – IC – YOU – LOUS.

Riddle-ic-you-lous is a made-up word. Here's how to say it: riddle – ICK – you – less.

If you're riddle-ic-you-lous, you'll read the riddle and cover up the answer while you try to work it out.

Or you could play a riddle-ic-you-lous game with a friend. You tell a riddle and they have to answer.

Then it's their turn to tell a riddle and your turn to guess the answer.

If the answer is right, the riddle-answering person gets 1 point. The person with the most points is the winner.

You could also play the riddle-ic-you-lous game with more than two people.

You might decide that an especially tricky, clever or beautiful riddle-ic-you-lous riddle deserves 2 points!

When you play riddle-ic-you-lous, you aren't playing to beat everybody else. It's more like you're a performer doing a jam session with words.

So, are you ready to fire up your riddle-ic-you-lous skills?

Turn the page and let's get this word party started!

Myles O'Smiles

1. My cities have no buildings,
my rivers have no water,
and my mountains have no trees.

What am I?

A map.

2. What has a foot at the bottom and a bottom at the top?

A leg.

3. You got this when you were born and will have it all your life.
You can't buy it, sell it or give it away.
Sometimes it's with you, and other times it's gone.

What is it?

Your shadow.

4. The more you take of these, the more you leave behind you.

What are they?

Footsteps.

5. You need to cross a river. You also want to get your dog, your chicken and a big bag of grain over to the other side of the river.

There is no bridge and no ferry. But you do have a rowboat.

Unfortunately, your boat is so small there's only room for you and one animal or thing in it. This means that you can't take the dog, the chicken and the grain with you at the same time while you row across the river.

You can't leave the dog alone with the chicken, because he's hungry and might eat the chicken. You can't leave the chicken alone with the bag of grain, because she is also hungry and will rip the bag open and start eating.

So how will you get everyone safely across the river?

You'll have to make three trips across the river.

On the first trip, leave the dog and the bag of grain and row across with the chicken. Leave the chicken on the other side of the river and return to where you started.

On your second trip, take the dog over, but bring the chicken back with you. Leave the chicken behind for your third trip, taking the grain to the other side. Then go back and, on your fourth and final time rowing across the river, take the chicken.

6. The Pickle family have two parents, one dog, 2 cats and 6 daughters.

The daughters are called Penny, Priscilla, Patty, Pamela, Peony and Petunia.

Each of these daughters has a brother.

How many Pickles are there in the Pickle family?

Twelve: 2 parents, 3 pets, 6 daughters and 1 son, Patrick, because he is a brother to all the Pickle girls.

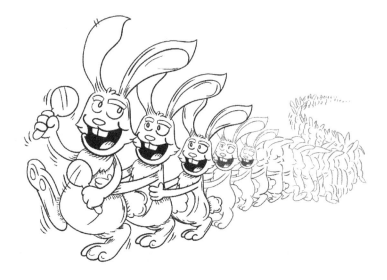

7. What do you call 20 rabbits in a row, when all of them are walking or dancing backwards?

A receding hare-line.

8. What is yellow and brown when you buy it, red when you use it and gray when it's time to throw it away?

Firewood.

9. I have a head and a foot, but four legs. What am I?

A bed.

10. I join 2 things together with a single bite. What am I?

A stapler.

11. I have 13 hearts, but no body and no brain. What am I?

A deck of cards.

12. I sit on top of your head, keeping it warm and dry, but I'm not a hat. What am I?

A roof.

13. What 5-letter word becomes shorter when you add 2 letters to it?

Short.

14. After booming and zapping is when I appear,
to bring you dazzling colors that shimmer so near.
Some say my end hides a pot of gold,
but those riches have rarely been found, so I'm told.

What am I?

A rainbow.

15. I have wings and I fly,
far and wide, through the skies.
You've probably seen me, soaring so high,

A miracle of flight, in day and night skies.

What am I?

An airplane.

16. Four bicycle repair people take 4 hours to repair 4 bicycles. If the bicycle shop owner hires 4 more repair workers, how long will it take all the bicycle repair people to repair 16 bicycles?

8 hours. Here's why. 4 bicycle repair people can repair 4 bicycles in 4 hours. Twice as many repair people – that's 8 - will repair twice as many bicycles – also 8 - in 4 hours. So, it will take these 8 bicycle repair people 8 hours to repair 16 bicycles.

17. What is hard to find and easy to lose?

A good friend.

18. Cats, dogs, birds, fish, leopard geckos, bearded dragons, snakes, hamsters, rabbits, gerbils and ponies are all animals that can be pets. What else do they all have in common?

The letter "s."

19. What always wears its feet on the inside?

A pair of shoes.

20. The Pickle family has 7 children. Patty Pickle is younger than her sister, Priscilla, but older than Pamela.

Patrick is older than Penny and Priscilla, who are both older than Patty. Peony is younger than Pamela, but older than Petunia. Patrick is older than Pamela. Who is the middle child in their family?

The middle child is Patty. Patrick is the oldest, then Priscilla, Penny, Patty, Pamela and, completing their family are Peony and Petunia. They're twins, but Petunia was born a few minutes after Peony, so Petunia is the youngest.

21. What's black and white and read all over?

The traditional answer to this very old riddle is "a newspaper" because it uses black ink on white paper and most adults read the newspaper, so it is "read all over." But a book with no pictures, printed with black ink on white paper and read all over the world is also a correct answer for this riddle.

22. Sometimes I have a hundred wheels, sometimes I have more, but sometimes I have none. What am I?

A parking lot.

23. You leave home, run as fast as you can, run to three places and then back to home, where there are two people wearing masks. Who are they?

The catcher and the umpire in a baseball game.

24. What do you call an investigator who can't solve any crimes?

A defective detective.

25. I'm black all over when you want to use me, And covered in white when you're done.

What am I?

A blackboard.

26. As soon as you say my name, I am broken.

What am I?

Silence.

27. What is something you used to have, but can never have again?

Yesterday.

28. What kind of key can open a banana?

A monkey.

29. What do you get in the middle of March or April that you don't see at the beginning, or the end, of either month?

The letter "r."

30. You see a ferry with lots of people on board. But when it lands, there isn't a single person on board! How could this happen?

All the passengers and crew are married.

31. How can your coat pocket be empty, but still have something in it?

It has a hole in it!

32. What is always promising to arrive, but never does?

The future.

33. I have three colourful eyes that tell you what to do.

What am I?

A traffic light.

34. I can hold water even though I'm full of holes.

What am I?

A sponge.

35. Throw away my outside, then you cook my inside. Then you eat the outside and throw away the inside.

What am I?

Corn on the cob.

36. I am round, hard, white or red and when you peel me, I know how to make you cry.

What am I?

An onion.

37. I am the white hem on the sea's blue skirt.
What am I?

A beach.

38. I am the black coat you drive on or walk on.
What am I?

Asphalt paving on a street or highway.

39. I carry power, marching across the countryside
and into towns and cities. What am I?

A pole line carrying wires for electricity.

40. Far from cities, I stand tall on hills, slowly
turning.

What am I?

Wind-mills generating wind power.

41. The Moon is my father,
the Ocean is my mother.
I have a billion brothers,
I travel to reach land, and there I vanish.

What am I?

A wave.

42. I have no voice, yet I can cry,
have no wings, but I can flutter,
have no teeth, but I can bite,
have no mouth, yet I can mutter.

What am I?

The wind.

43. I scream, I soar, I seek the sky
with flowers of fire I fly high.
I'm an Eastern art, from an ancient time.
My name will solve this riddle rhyme.

What am I?

Fireworks.

44. Here's a question the Mad Hatter asks Alice
during the tea party in Alice in Wonderland. Alice
doesn't know the answer to this riddle. Do you?

"Why is a raven like a writing desk?"

Because both have a "n" and neither has an "b."

And here's another clever answer:

A writing desk is a rest for pens and a raven is a pest for wrens.

45. I have a neck but no head,
shoulders but no arms,
a bottom but no legs or feet
and you can see right through me.

What am I?

A bottle.

46. I turn everything around, right to left or left to right. But I never move.

What am I?

A mirror.

47. You are a business person who is travelling when you come to a fork in the road. Each fork leads to a village. In one village, you've heard that everyone always lies. The other fork leads to a village where everyone always tells the truth.

You want to do business with the honest village people, but you don't know which village this is. Then, you see a man from one of the villages and you stop to ask for directions. He tells you he will answer just one question. But you don't know which village he comes from. Maybe he's an honest villager...or maybe not.

What one simple question can you ask him that will help you find the honest villagers?

Here is the question to ask: "Which road goes to your village?" Then, take the road that he points to because you can be sure it is the road to the truthful village. Here's why: a truthful person will point to his own village, the truthful village. A liar would also point to the truthful village since he is a liar and so he wouldn't point to his own village.

48. Your friend tells you that she can throw a ball a short distance so that it will come to a complete stop, then reverse the direction it's going in.

She says she can do this without throwing the ball against a wall or bouncing it on the ground. And the ball won't have a string, or elastic, or anything attached to it.

How is this possible?

Your friend can do this by throwing the ball straight up in the air.

49. I have been with you for all your life,
and I'll always walk beside you.
You can't see me or touch me, hear me or smell me...
Yet you know I'm always with you.

When you're very young, you might have too much of me.
When you're older, you might have too little.

You might wish I'd hurry up...
you might wish I'd slow down.
But nothing you can do will change what I am
because I am unchanged and unchanging forever.

What am I?

Time.

50. What is half of two plus two?

Three. Half of two is one. One plus two is three.

51. You can write this word upside down or even backwards and it's still exactly the same word. What is it?

swims.

52. Five of your friends are eating apples after lunch. Alice finished her apple before Barbara did, but after Carl. Donna finished before Emily, but after Barbara.

What order did these friends finish eating, from first to last?

Carl finished first. Then, in order, Alice, Barbara and Donna. Emily finished her apple last.

53. I have a ring, but no fingers,
I hear voices, but can't talk,
I go where you go,
or sit at home in my dock.
I have a window but no door.
I have keys and a lock.
What am I?

A cell-phone.

54. I'm green, with four leaves.
Some people say finding me is lucky.
This may be true, especially if you're Irish!

What am I?

A shamrock.

55. I have space but no room,
keys and a lock,
numbers, signs and symbols,
26 letters but no stamps,
a home and control
and I do nothing until you plug me in.
But if it all goes wrong, I offer an escape.

What am I?

A keyboard.

56. First you see me in the grass
dressed in yellow gay;
Next I am in dainty white,
then I fly away.

What am I?

A dandelion.

57. She has hands that do not hold,
she has teeth that cannot bite.
She has feet, but they are cold,
she has eyes, but has no sight.

Who is she?

A doll.

58. He will run forever,
but never move at all.
He has no lips, no mouth, no throat or lungs,
but still a roaring call.

What is he?

A waterfall.

59. Never resting, never still.
Moving silently from field to hill.
I never walk, run or trot.
Everything is cool where I am not.

What am I?

Sunshine.

60. You throw this out when you need it,
and take it in when you don't.
What is it?

An anchor.

61. You can hear this sing, with its hard tongue.
It cannot breathe, it has no lungs.

What is it?

A bell.

62. When you buy a car, you get this, even if you don't want it.
It's no use to you or to the car, but a car can't go anywhere without it.

What is it?

Noise.

63. You are in a room with a monkey, a gorilla and an orangutan. One of them is eating a banana, one has a stick and is using it to scratch his back, and one is playing with a ball. Who is the smartest primate in the room?

You are.

64. I can dance and play
on a breezy day.
I live in the sky,
but sleep on the ground.

What am I?

A kite.

65. I'm an animal you might sleep with tonight.
If you do, when you wake up I will have vanished
without a trace.

What am I?

A nightmare.

66. I have a hundred skinny legs, but do not stand
on my own.
I have a long neck, but no head.
I can't see, hear or smell,
but I'm tidy as can be.

What am I?

A broom.

67. This is a mile from end to end,
yet as close to you as your best friend.
Anyone can give it, no one can buy it.
Even when you're sad, you can try it.

Doesn't matter if you're rich, poor, short or tall.
But shared among children most of all.
Everyone can do it, and you might, too

when the answer to this riddle is revealed to YOU.
What is it?

A smile!

68. Sometimes I'm quiet, sometimes I'm loud.
Take away my eye and I'm on the front of your face.

What am I?

Noise. Take away the "i" for nose.

69. Sometimes I'm white but I'm always wrong.
I break hearts and hurt even the strong.
I can build anything up or tear it down.
I might make you smile, but more likely a frown.

What am I?

A lie.

70. I describe where animals sleep.
Take one letter away, and I'm where you eat.
Take another away, and I'm strong and capable.
Do you think that now you can solve this riddle?

What word am I?

Stable – table – able.

71. I'm flat as paper,
round as a ring.
Though I have two eyes,
I can't see a thing.

What am I?

A button.

72. My marble halls are white as milk,
lined with a skin as soft as silk.
No doors there are to this stronghold,
yet thieves break in and steal the gold.

What am I?

An egg.

73. I dig out tiny caves and store gold and silver in them.
I build bridges of silver and make crowns of gold.
Everything I build is the smallest you could imagine.
Everyone needs my help, but many fear me.

Who am I?

A dentist.

74. When I am warm, I gently caress your skin.
When I am hot, I rise to the sky.

When cold, I can crack rocks and sink ships.

What am I?

Water – when it is liquid, a gas, and frozen into ice.

75. Poor people have this,
rich people need this,
happy people desire this,
misers spend this,
spenders save this.
And when your life is over, this is what you'll own.

What is it?

Nothing.

76. Called by the moon,
in we go, out we go.
All around and in a row.
Sometimes high and sometimes low.
Always, always steady flow.
We started this so long ago
our true age, no one knows.
Today, tomorrow and forever,
in we go, out we go.

What are we?

Ocean tides.

77. I rarely leave my native land.
For all my life, straight I stand.
High and low I may be found.
Growing above and below ground.

What am I?

A tree. The part of a tree you see above ground is as big as the tree's root system hidden below ground.

78. In bed at night you turn and toss.
With stories true or stories false,
awake, you might forget their power,
asleep, they rule you, head and heart.

What are they?

Your dreams.

79. She has 1 and so does he, we, I, or eye.
Person has 2 and citizen has 3.
Human being has 4.
Personality has 5.
6 is for an inhabitant of earth.
Astronomers study stars is 7
Aliens who live on spaceships is 8.
Astronauts who explore outer space is 9.
Do you think there are other worlds like Earth? is 10.

What are they?

Syllables.

80. What will you find in the middle of nowhere?

The letter "h." And here's another tricky thing about this word. When you break it in two, you get "now here."

81. What force and strength cannot get through
with gentle touch I will do.
Many in the street would continue to stand
were I not a friend they can hold in their hand.

What am I?

Door keys to homes.

82. Two brothers are we.
Great burdens we bear.
Yet this I will say,
we are full all through the day
and empty when finally, we rest.

What are we?

A pair of work boots.

83. They can be harbored,
but few hold water.
You can nurse them,
but only by holding them
against someone else.
You can carry them,
but not with your arms.
You can bury them,
but not in the earth.

What are they?

Grudges.

84. By Moon or by Sun,
I can be found.

Yet I am undone,
when there's no light around.

What am I?

Your shadow.

85. Larger than a mountain,
or smaller than a pea,
I'm endlessly swimming
in a dark, waterless sea.

What am I?

An asteroid.

86. We don't breathe,
but we run and jump.
We don't eat,
but we swim and stretch.
We don't drink,
but we sleep and stand.
We don't think,
but we grow and play.
We don't see, but you see us every day.

What are we?

Your legs.

87. What do you call a nut cracker up a tree?

A squirrel.

88. When water splashes me,
none can get through.

When I am moved a lot,
moisture I spew.

When I am hit,
color I change.

And for color myself, I come in a wide range.
What I cover is very complex

and your last hint is this: I'm easy to flex.

What am I?

Your skin.

89. When you're given 1,
you'll have 2 or none.
Vanilla or chocolate?
Reading or bed?
Sometimes this
is all in your head.

What is it?

Choice.

90. The more of it there is, the less you will see,

What is it?

Darkness.

91. Face like a tree,
skin like the sea.
A smart creature I am,
yet ants frighten me.

What am I?

An elephant.

92. I'm all over your head,
but under your hat.

What am I?

Your hair.

93. My voice is tender,
my waist is slender,
I'm often invited to play.
Yet wherever I go,
I must take my bow
or else I have nothing to say.

What am I?

A violin, or fiddle.

94. Lovely and round,
I shine with pale light.
Grown in the ocean's darkness,
I'm a lady's delight.

What am I?

A pearl.

95. The strangest bird you'll ever find,
I've got two eyes in front
and a hundred behind.

What am I?

A peacock.

96. I open wide
but then snap shut.
Sharp am I when paper I cut.
Fingers too, so please take care,
I'm good and bad, so it's smart to beware!

What am I?

Scissors.

97. I can be false or true,
written or spoken.
I can be revealed and exposed,
and I'm often broken.
What am I?

The daily news.

98. These start out green,
then later they're brown.
Both of these times,
if you eat them, you'll frown.

But just in between,
for a very short while,
they're perfect and yellow.
When you taste them, you'll smile!

What are they?

Bananas.

99. A little house with 2 inside.
But sometimes 1, and rarely 3.
Break the walls and seeds.
Then throw away the walls!

What am I?

A peanut.

100. I have many of these.
So do you.
Take away 1 and a bit remains.
Take away 2 and bit remains.
Take away 3 and it remains.

What am I?

The word "habit."

101. These glittering points grow downwards.
Sharp as spears, they never rust.

What are they?

Icicles.

102. 1 in window but not in pane.
2 in road but not in lane.
3 in oval but not in round
4 in hearing but not in sound.
Together I'm a sign of peace,
from Noah's ark won quick release.

What am I?

A dove. This riddle is tricky because it hints at the letters in d-o-v-e. The first letter, "D" is in window but not pane. Get it?

103. Give me a smile and I'll always smile back.

What am I?

A mirror.

104. Snake twisted and coiled
round and round.
Snake used above board
and to climb mountains
or explore caves under ground.
Snake that never has head or tail.
Snake that ties and binds
used on boats that sail.

What am I?

Rope.

105. Begins with 1 in ocean but never in sea.
The second is in wasp but never in bee.
The last is in glider and also in flight.
I'm a shy creature that comes out at night.

What am I?

An owl.

106. I am the ocean's teeth.
Feared by sailors.
Ridden by bears.
Towering above,
Yet most of me is hidden beneath.

What am I?

An iceberg.

107. There is 1 in the corner.
There are 2 in this room.
3 in booklover
4 in stone soup and spoon.

What am I?

The letter "o."

108. Just 3 little letters.
A paradox to some.
The worse that it is,
the more it is fun!

What is it?

A pun.

109. Almost everyone wants to give this.
Almost no one wants to take it.
Even when it's exactly what they need the most.

What is it?

Advice.

110. I'm a god of the ancients
and a planet near the sun.
I measure heat or cold.
Another name for me is quicksilver.

What am I?

Mercury.

111. What always goes up and never comes down?

Your age.

112. We are always around you, though sunlight makes us invisible.

What are we?

Stars in the sky.

113. I'm a tempting snack,
that's juicy, sweet and good to eat.
I also help protect your teeth.
I have a shiny coat of red
or green or maybe golden yellow.

What am I?

An apple.

114. We are five little objects of an everyday sort.
You will find us in order in a tennis court.

What are we?

Vowels – a, e, i, o and u.

115. Who works when he plays,
and plays when he works?

A musician.

116. You might catch me, especially in cold weather. But you can never throw me.

What am I?

A cold.

117. You put this coat on when it's wet
and enjoy seeing it when it's dry.
It can last a long time.
But when you get tired of it, you just put another coat on top.

What is it?

A coat of paint.

118. I can make every word in many languages, but I cannot speak.

What am I?

The alphabet.

119. I go up when the rain comes down,
I go down when the sun comes out.

What am I?

An umbrella.

120. I'm bought by the yard or the metre, but always worn by the foot.

What am I?

A carpet.

121. What do you swallow every day that can also swallow you, if you aren't careful?

Water.

122. You use me every day,
from your head to your toes.
And the more you use me,
the smaller I grow.

What am I?

A bar of soap.

123. I sleep a lot.
I flick my tail when I'm angry,
and hum when I'm glad.
I can jump further and higher than you can,
and protect your home from pests.

What am I?

A cat.

124. Grown on hillsides.
Eaten by many.
White as snow.
An ideal food!

What is it?

Rice.

125. I live next to a beauty.
She's trying to catch your eye.
If you grab me without looking,
you're surely going to cry.

What am I?

A thorn on a rosebush.

126. I have no feathers and no wings
but I can still fly.
By my wind and my noise,
you'll know I'm hovering nearby.

What am I?

A helicopter.

127. Tickle me with your fingers
and a song I will sing.

But if you aren't careful,
You could break a string.

What am I?

A guitar. Or a ukulele, mandolin or autoharp.

128. This can move you,
or it can make you move.
You can't touch it, taste it or smell it,
but you'll know it's there
And you'll miss it, once it's gone.
Many people can't live without it.

What is it?

Music.

129. I stand upright and tall,
or can be quite grand.
My strings are hidden,
my keys under your hands.

What am I?

A piano.

130. I've got words, and words, and words, and
more words.
Some of them, you've never heard!

What am I?

A dictionary.

131. I'm a bright flash of light
On a gray day.
If you're wood or you're metal,
you'd best stay away!

What am I?

Lightning.

132. I met a boy and drew his name,
he stopped a while, we played a game.
Now can you tell me
What's this boy's name?

His name is Andrew.

133. I have every colour and many different shapes.
You won't see what I am until you fit my shapes
together.
You can do this any way you want, but there is only
one way that works.

What am I?

A jigsaw puzzle.

134. I protect you by sitting on a bridge.
You can see right through me, but others can't.
I have two arms that hug you.

What am I?

Your sunglasses.

135. Some like me hot, some like me cold.
Some prefer mild, some prefer bold.
I'm made from a bean.
I help people wake up.
What am I?

Coffee.

136. Throw me off the tallest building and I'll simply
float away.
Throw me in the ocean and I won't last one day.
Put me in your pocket. That's where I'm usually
found,
pull me out to use me, I won't make a sound.

What am I?

A tissue.

139. I have 21 black eyes that do not see.
There are six white sides of me.
You'll always find me with my twin.

Shake us up and you could win!

What are we?

A pair of dice.

140. I'm a plant that likes to climb.
My name has 3 letters.
The first 2 letters say my name.
The last letter asks a question.

What plant am I?

Ivy.

141. I was invented long ago in China.
I carry some of the world's most precious things,
yet anyone can own me.
You use me every day.
You might be looking at me, right now.

What am I?

Paper.

142. What word becomes smaller when you make it longer?

Small.

143. Chicken + pig + plate.

What am I?

Bacon and eggs.

144. Give this, and you must keep it.
Receive this with gratitude.
Treasure this always.

What is it?

A promise.

145. Puffy white,
your mouth's delight.
I start from a golden seed.
But over heat

I become a movie treat!

What am I?

Popcorn

146. I ask no questions
but always demand an answer.

What am I?

A phone.

147. I've driven people mad for the love of me.
Everyone has me but I'm never free.

What am I?

Money.

148. People and animals make this all the time.
So do cars, planes, trains and machines.
You can't see it, touch it, taste it or smell it.
But when it's there, you can't ignore it.

What is it?

Noise.

149. At night, we come out

all on our own.
By day we have vanished
without being stolen.

What are we?

The moon, planets and stars in the sky.

150. When you take off your clothes,
it puts them on.
When it takes them off,
you put them on.

What is it?

A clothes hangar.

151. I come in many colours, styles and sizes
but I'm always only 1 foot long.

What am I?

A shoe.

152. I stick to many things, but I'm not sticky at all.

What am I?

A magnet.

153. You can bat me,
but I never get a hit.
I help protect a ball
that's never thrown.

What am I?

Your eyelashes.

154. Born of troubles,
increasing with age.
You need a lot of this
to be a sage.

What am I?

Wisdom.

155. People throw me,
dogs catch me,
though I'm round, I'm not a ball.

What am I?

A frisbee.

156. You might like me,
or maybe not.
I'm old-fashioned
and always dated.

What am I?

History.

157. Where does yesterday follow today?

In the dictionary.

158. Never ahead, forever behind,
flying swiftly past.
If you're a child, I last forever,
for adults, I'm gone too fast.

What am I?

Youth (the ages from 12 to 20).

159. Funny funny words words words words.

What does this mean?

2 funny 4 words.

160. Dice dice.

What does this mean?

Pair-a-dice.

161. _____ travel.

What does this mean?

Space travel.

162. 2nd 2 0

What does this mean?

Second to none.

163. sta4nce

What does this mean?

For instance.

164. 3 ends 57 ends 83 ends 115 ends.

What does this mean?

Odds and ends.

165. I'm a kind of weather
that often comes your way.
But add one letter
and now I run away.

What am I?

Rain - a drain.

166. I'm a path between mountains.
But take away one letter
and I'm found in every city.

What am I?

A valley.

167. Delicate, fragile on the wing.
You'll say I am a pretty thing.
I stop and visit many flowers,
I must hide when there are showers.

What am I?

A butterfly.

168. Glass beads scattered over the grass and in the meadow, just as the sun awakens.

What is it?

Dew.

169. Boys want it, but most men don't. Every morning, they remove it, but it's back again tomorrow. What is it?

Whiskers, or a beard.

170. Bbride

What does this mean?

Bride-to-be.

171. A sandy place, where few can live.
Often hot and always dry.
My name means "to leave."
It's not hard to see why.

What am I?

A desert.

172. Be sure to shout!
Its answers are weak.
But there's no language,

it cannot speak!

What is it?

An echo.

173. BIG BIG ignore ignore

What does this mean?
Too big to ignore.

174. Ca Ca Ca Ca Ca Ca Ca Ca Ca

What does this mean?

Canine.

175. cycle cycle cycle

What does this mean?

A tricycle.

176. I can honk without a horn.
When I grow up I grow down.
You might see me in farmers' fields
or flying in a V above you.

What am I?

A goose.

177. I have a strong backbone,
but not any legs.
I peel like an orange,
but come from an egg.

What am I?

*A snake. It peels each time it sheds its skin, allowing
it to grow larger.*

178. I'm a constant collector
of sweet flower nectar.
I'm a bird, not a bee.
Flying so fast, I'm hard to see.

What am I?

A hummingbird.

179. Pawalkrk

What does this mean?

A walk in the park.

180. Welcomed by farmers and gardeners.
Spoiler of picnics and playing outside.
Cooler and smoother than any rhyme.

Loves to fall but can never climb.

What is it?

Rain.

181. Seven sisters are we.
For 5 we work all day.
The other 2 are for errands and play.

What are we?

Days of the week.

182. There are 10 parts of the human body whose names each have only 3 letters. Can you name all 10?

They are: ear, eye, lip, hip, toe, arm, leg, jaw, gum and rib.

183. We wait through many cold days and nights for this.
The richest person can't buy it.
But when it finally arrives, it's free for all to enjoy.

What is it?

Springtime.

184. Child or adult, boy or girl,
everyone gets excited when this time comes.

When is it?

Time for vacation!

185. Everyone does this.
Most people worry about it.
But some people enjoy it.
Almost everyone prepares for it.
What is this?

Taking a test or exam.

186. A time of giving and receiving,
singing and feasting.
A time to rejoice,
with family and friends.

When is this?

A holiday, such as Thanksgiving, Hanukah or Christmas.

187. Lying in the sun,
a picnic at the beach.
Time to read, or explore,
ice cream for a treat.

When is this?

Summer vacation.

188. The edge of earth and a loaf of bread.

What is it?

The crust.

189. The older they get,
the less wrinkles they have.
Until finally they are completely smooth.

What are they?

Tires.

190. There's no country on earth,
where I haven't travelled countless times.
No one knows where I was born,
but when I come you'll know my roar.
Whether it be day or night,
I neither am nor can be seen.

What am I?

The wind.

191. Two in every deck of cards,

one in a famous movie.

What and who am I?

The Joker.

192. What is the beginning of all that ends?

Birth.

193. What is the first thing every gardener plants in their garden?

Their feet.

194. I'm in the middle of water, but I'm not an island.

What am I?

The letter "t."

195. I sit when I stand.
Jump when I walk.
Climb when I'm born.
And I can't talk.

What am I?

A kangaroo.

196. I'm a cup that can't hold a drink.
And something you'd love to find in your lunchbox.

What am I?

A cupcake.

197. I'm chewy, or crispy.
I'm always round,
and usually sweet.

What am I?

A cookie.

198. One year in four
I leap to 29.

What am I?

February 29th in a Leap Year.

199. Head of lamb,
center of pig,
hind of buffalo,
tail of dragon.
Call me King!

What am I?

A lion, king of the cat family.

200. I look heavy, but I'm light.
I'm rarely seen at night.
I'm fat, fluffy and white.
I draw pictures in the sky.

What am I?

Clouds.

201. Your head would fall off and roll away if you
didn't have this.

What is it?

Your neck.

202. One way it's a number,
spell it backwards and it catches things.

What is it?

Ten.

203. By day I have just 4 legs but by night I have 6.

What am I?

Your bed.

204. I have a red head,
green hair,
a long white beard,
and no body.

What am I?

A radish.

205. You deal with us and we deal in chance,
we might show your future at a glance.
You play with us and we play you back,
then, win, lose or draw,
we hop back in our pack.

What are we?

A deck of cards.

206. I am dark.
But combine me with paper
and I can enlighten the world.

What am I?

Ink.

207. I have no beginning,
I have no end.
I have many flavours
and sometimes, I have sprinkles.

What am I?

Donuts.

208. What do you call a foot covering that is long
and slippery?

A slipper.

209. Rude to you I will never be
though I show my tongue for all to see.

Who am I?

Your dog.

210. Weight in my belly,

trees on my back,
nails in my ribs,
feet I do lack.

What am I?

A sailing ship.

211. I don't work unless I'm sharp.
I only work when there's something in my eye.

What am I?

A needle.

212. This is an age that all travellers have.

What is it?

Baggage.

213. Thirty men and ladies two,
gathered for a festive do.
Dressed quite formally, black and white.
Soon movement turns to all in flight.

What is this?

A game of chess.

214. Red on black and black on red,
seven stacks with four above.
Numbers high to numbers low.
A game of chance to pass the time.

What am I?

A game of Solitaire, also known as Klondike or Patience.

215. Spibred.

What does this mean?

Be inspired.

216.

What does this mean?

Flowery speech.

217. Sir Lance. Sir Lance. Sir Lance.

What does this mean?

Sir Lancelot.

218. Zero soon soon.

What does this mean?

None too soon.

219. Lannnnguage.

What does this mean?

Foreign language. (4-n language).

220. LIFE live live.

What does this mean?

One life to live.

221. Red, pink or white,
gardeners' delight!
Sometimes orange or yellow,
smelling sweet or mellow.
A part of me can make a tea
healthy because it's got Vitamin C.

What are we?

Roses. (The tea is made from rosehips)

222. I'm not a chair, couch or stool,

not a loveseat or a recliner.
Yet I'm useful to sit on
wherever you are.

What am I?

A bench.

223. Green leaves, white petals, yellow centre.
Often seen in meadows.
People call me the most cheerful of flowers.

What am I?

A daisy.

224. I hang below a tree,
serving tiny meals to all who visit.

What am I?

A birdfeeder.

225. I am plants, but not trees.
Growing thick, you can't see through me.
I stand tall in a line along a boundary.
Everywhere you look, you might find me
in villages, towns and cities and even out in the
country.

What am I?

A hedge.

226. When I'm liquid, don't touch me, or I will hurt you.
When I'm solid, if you touch me, be careful!
I'm useful for holding things and looking through,
An ancient discovery, made of sand.

What am I?

Glass.

227. I'm made of glass, metal, wood, beads or jewels.
All I want to do is make you look good.
Some people want me,
some use me,
some trade me,
some sell me.
Some call me "treasure," and sometimes I'm famous.

What am I?

Jewellery.

228. They look at problems from every angle.
Always looking for solutions,
seeking answers for mankind.

Who are they?

Scientists.

229. How many 9s are there between 8 and 100?

Twenty. Here they are: 9, 19, 29, 39, 49, 59, 69, 79, 89, 90, 91, 92, 93, 94, 95, 96, 97, 98 and there are two in 99.

230. Looks like water.
Created by heat.
Sits on sand,
lays on concrete.

Ahead on the road,
a play on tired eyes,
but you soon realize
It's just lies.

What is it?

A mirage.

231. Give give give give and get get get get
What does this mean?

Forgive and forget.

232. A short green plant, always thirsty.
Surrounding many houses and maybe yours?

What is it?

Grass.

233. We sing in the morning.
Fly all day.
Sleep at night.
And every year we travel vast distances.

What are we?

Songbirds.

234. You work at this all day
dreaming of when it's time to play.
You might play at this later
with computer, pen or paper.

What is it?

Your desk.

235. Ci-ring rc-ring us-ring.

What does this mean?

Three-ring circus.

236. Efliegsn.

Unscramble this word to find out what it means.

Mixed feelings.

237. All.
Again.

What does this mean?

All over again.

238. They help us experience our world
in fresh new ways we might never have thought of.

They open our eyes to new visions of ourselves.

Who are they?

Artists.

239. They are the master builders.
They design machines that can
improve our lives.
Their tools are steel, glass, wood
and computers.

Who are they?

Engineers.

240. They guide us as we grow in knowledge and
experience.
We could not become masters of anything without
them.

Who are they?

Teachers.

241. They rush to us in times of trouble.
They rescue us when we're afraid.
They always announce their presence.
They're always ready to help, day or night.

Who are they?

Emergency workers, including search and rescue teams, ambulance drivers and firefighters.

242. We don't always like them, but we always need them.
They give us leadership.
Many seek this powerful job; few hold it.

Who are they?

Political leaders.

243. Their job is to serve and protect.
They work long hours to provide law and order.

Who are they?

Police.

244. No one wants to meet with them,
yet after they do, everyone is glad they did.
They wear a white uniform,
they know everything about one small part of your body.

Who are they?

Dentists.

245. Without them, you would have no movies to watch,
and no books to read (not even this one!)

Who are they?

Writers.

246. You would become very hungry if there were none of these.

Who are they?

Farmers.

247. Businesses rely on these to keep track of the money,
what they've sold, and what they're owed.

Who are they?

Accountants.

248. This is one of the most difficult jobs there is, the hours are long, and there is no pay.
Yet millions of people have this job, and millions more want it.

What is it?

Being parents.

249. When we're sick, we wait to see them, when we're well we stay away.

Who are they?

Doctors and nurses.

250. They keep everyone focused on a goal, and help others do their best possible work.

Who are they?

Business managers.

251. They snip and clip
to keep you looking well-groomed.
Once you leave their chairs,

they tidy up with their brooms.

Who are they?

Hairdressers and barbers.

252. Inside me stories, pictures and adventures you'll find,
quests and treasures of every kind!
When you wish to visit you'll soon see,
your hands are the key that unlock me.
And here's one more hint to help you this time,
helpfully placed near the end of this rhyme.
The word that's my name begins with a "b."
You'll spend happy hours, inside of me!

What am I?

A book, like this one!

How to Write a Riddle

Reading and sharing riddles isn't the *only* way to have fun with them! You could also write some riddles!

Ready to give it a go?

It's easy when you know the secret to riddle writing. And here is that secret. Start with the answer. Then think up all your clues and turn your best clues into a tricky question. Your question might rhyme, but it doesn't have to!

Let's say you want to write a riddle about playing with Lego® building blocks. That's the answer to your riddle; Legos®.

So now, think about what would describe what it's like to play with Legos®.

- They're colourful.
- They're plastic.
- They snap together.
- Kids love playing with them all over the world.
- You can build space ships or castles or an entire city or anything at all with them!
- One boy recently built a huge model of the Titanic with Legos®!

Grab a piece of paper and a pen and write down every single thing you know about playing with Legos (or you could do this on your computer). You want a long list with LOTS of clues to add to the ones in the list here!

Use your clever clues list to create your riddle question. Remember, make it mysterious! It's more fun if it isn't *too* easy to guess!

So…how did you do? Do you like your riddle? Give it a try on your family and friends! They might have suggestions for how you can make your new riddle even MORE riddle-ic-you-lous!

You can go back through this book any time, or many times if you want to for fun and for inspiration to write your own riddles.

I hope you've had lots of fun with these riddles and sharing them with your family and friends!

Myles O'Smiles

That's all, Kids!

THANKS for reading!

About the Author

Myles O'Smiles is a former teacher and current book writer who believes that the very best way to learn something is when you enjoy it. His mission is to make kids laugh while they learn!

He lives with his family in a treehouse, where he enjoys anything that's silly, taking long elderberry tea breaks, gazing out at the stars and thinking up new word game and activity books for kids.

Here are all the books he's written, so far:

- Fun Jokes for Funny Kids
- Clever Scenarios for Clever Kids
- Awesome Riddles for Awesome Kids
- More Fun Jokes, Riddles and Scenarios for Happy Kids

All of them are available on Amazon or you can find out more by going to the Myles O'Smiles website at:

www.MylesOSmiles.com

You can also write to Myles and tell him your favorite joke!

Also, some of the funny images in this book are now on T-Shirts. Check out the Myles O'Smiles website or look for Crimson Hill Creations on Etsy to find out more.

www.MylesOSmiles.com

Made in the USA
Monee, IL
11 December 2019